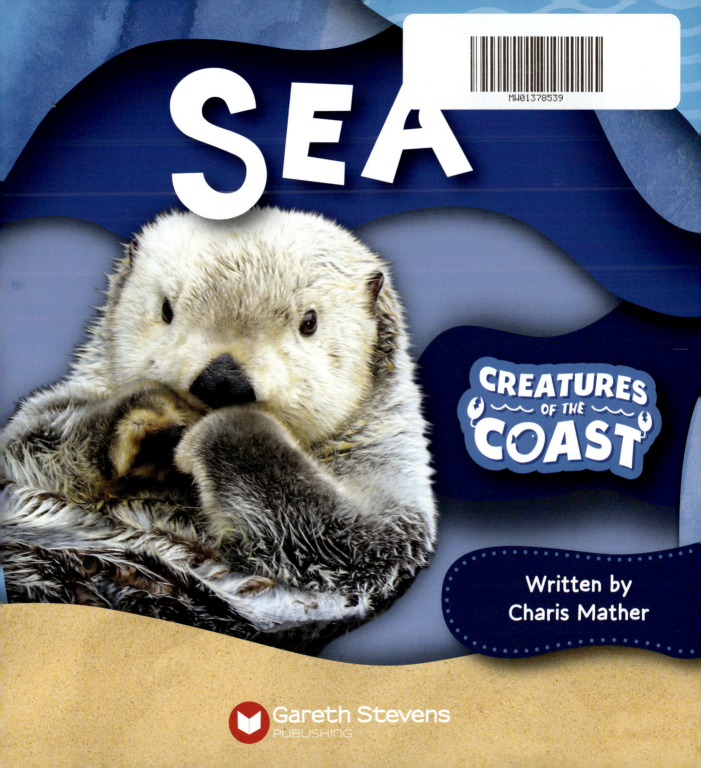

SEA

CREATURES OF THE COAST

Written by
Charis Mather

Gareth Stevens
PUBLISHING

Please visit our website, www.garethstevens.com. For a free color catalog of all our high-quality books, call toll free 1-800-542-2595 or fax 1-877-542-2596.

Published in 2025 by
Gareth Stevens Publishing
2544 Clinton St.
Buffalo, NY 14224

Written by:
Charis Mather

Edited by:
Rebecca Phillips-Bartlett

Designed by:
Amy Li

Cataloging-in-Publication Data

Names: Mahter, Charis.
Title: Sea / Charis Mahter.
Description: New York : Gareth Stevens Publishing, 2025. | Series: Creatures of the coast | Includes glossary and index.
Identifiers: ISBN 9781538294710 (pbk.) | ISBN 9781538294727 (library bound) | ISBN 9781538294734 (ebook)
Subjects: LCSH: Marine animals--Juvenile literature. | Marine ecology--Juvenile literature.
Classification: LCC QL122.2 M384 2025 | DDC 591.77--dc23

© 2023 Booklife Publishing

This edition is published by arrangement with Booklife Publishing

All rights reserved. No part of this book may be reproduced in any form without permission in writing from the publisher, except by a reviewer.

Printed in the United States of America

CPSIA compliance information: Batch #CSGS25: For further information contact Gareth Stevens at 1-800-542-2595.

Find us on

PHOTO CREDITS: All images courtesy of Shutterstock. With thanks to Getty Images, Thinkstock Photo and iStockphoto.
Recurring images: etcberry, Luria, GoodStudio, Lexi Claus, Baskiabat, Net Vector, Perfect_kebab, MR. BUDDEE WIANGNGORN. Cover – A. Kiro, abrakadabra, nvphoto, 2–3 – Andrea Izzotti. 4–5 – divedog, Ethan Daniels, jejim, Vlad61. 6–7 – John A. Anderson, Peter Leahy. 8–9 – Magicleaf, Mariusz S. Jurgielewicz, Wirestock Creators. 10–11 – liu yu shan, Marcos del Mazo, Yauheniya Krupel. 12–13 – Daryl Duda, frantisekhojdysz. 14–15 – Gerald Peplow, RLS Photo, Nora Hachio. 16–17 – Gertjan Hooijer, lattesmile, yhelfman. 18–19 – GoodStudio, RMMPPhotography, Tory Kallman. 20–21 – JungleOutThere, VanekPhoto_21, worldswildlifewonders. 22–23 – Don Pablo, Vlad61.

CONTENTS

Page 4	In the Sea
Page 6	Corals
Page 8	Jellyfish
Page 10	Seahorses
Page 12	Fish
Page 14	Lobsters
Page 16	Seals
Page 18	Dolphins
Page 20	Sea Otters
Page 22	Creatures of the Coast
Page 24	Glossary and Index

Words that look like this can be found in the glossary on page 24.

In The Sea

Most of our planet is covered with water. Many of the creatures that live in the seas and oceans make their homes near the coasts. Coasts are where the land meets the sea.

Seagrasses, kelps, and coral reefs are often found in the shallow waters near the coasts. These shallow waters are great places for many coastal creatures to find food and hide from predators.

KELP

CORAL REEF

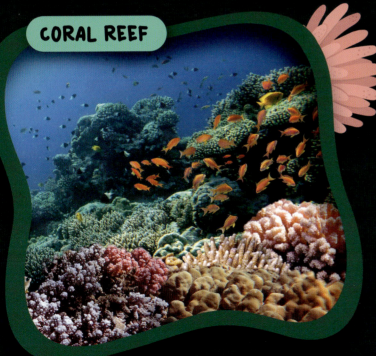

SEAGRASS

CORALS

BOULDER STAR CORAL

POLYPS

Corals may look like lumps of rock, but they are actually made up of tiny animals called polyps. The polyps grow hard, protective skeletons around themselves.

Corals come in many different colors, shapes, and sizes. When lots of corals grow in the same place, they form coral reefs. Many sea creatures live in and around coral reefs.

STAGHORN CORAL

JELLYFISH

TENTACLE

SEA NETTLE JELLYFISH

Jellyfish are not actually fish. They are squishy creatures whose bodies are made mostly of water. Unlike fish, jellyfish do not have bones, blood, hearts or even eyes. Instead of legs or tails, jellyfish have tentacles.

Jellyfish use their tentacles to protect themselves and to sting prey. Some jellyfish stings can be very painful to humans. Other stings are not strong enough for humans to feel at all.

Jellyfish often get washed up onto beaches by the waves.

SEAHORSES

FIN

SNOUT

Seahorses are small sea creatures with snouts and long, curly tails. Seahorses eat by sucking prey through their snouts. They swim using the small fins on their backs.

Seahorses are often found living in coral reefs or beds of seagrass. To keep themselves safe from predators, seahorses can change the color of their skin to match what is around them.

LONGSNOUT SEAHORSES

WHEN ANIMALS BLEND IN WITH THEIR SURROUNDINGS, THIS IS CALLED CAMOUFLAGE.

FISH

HOGFISH

There are thousands of different kinds of saltwater fish. Many of these fish live near coasts where the water is often warmer and there is a lot of food.

Sharks are a type of fish. Many sharks look after their young in nurseries near shallow coastal waters. Young sharks are protected by underwater plant life such as mangrove roots.

LEMON SHARK

LOBSTERS

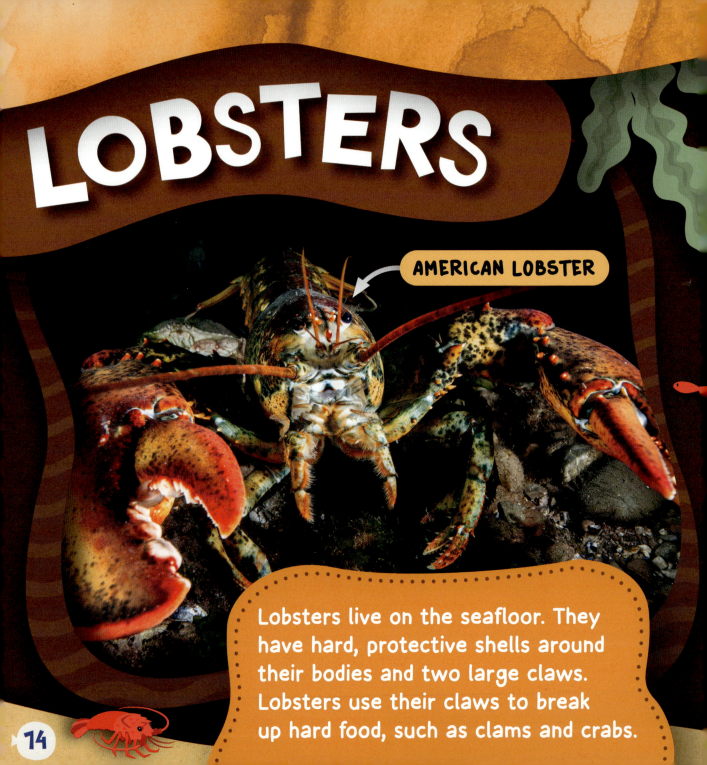

AMERICAN LOBSTER

Lobsters live on the seafloor. They have hard, protective shells around their bodies and two large claws. Lobsters use their claws to break up hard food, such as clams and crabs.

When lobsters are ready to grow, they have to squirm out of their old shells. This is called molting. After molting, lobsters grow new, larger shells around themselves.

A LOBSTER SHELL LEFT BEHIND AFTER MOLTING

SEALS

HARBOR SEAL

Many seals spend a lot of time in the sea. Their fin-shaped feet make them excellent swimmers. Seals can dive underwater for a long time before they need to come up for air.

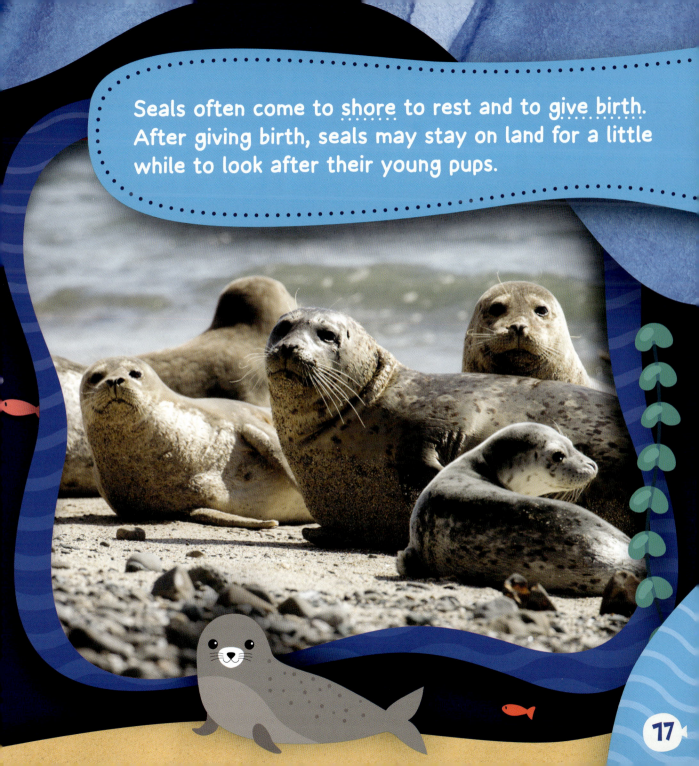

Seals often come to shore to rest and to give birth. After giving birth, seals may stay on land for a little while to look after their young pups.

DOLPHINS

BLOWHOLE

Dolphins can be found all over the world. Dolphins are mammals. They need to breathe air to live. Dolphins can sometimes be spotted coming out of the water for air.

Dolphins breathe through blowholes on their heads.

Dolphins usually swim together in groups called pods. They are social animals and enjoy playing. Dolphins may chase each other, play with things they find in the ocean, or make up new games.

COMMON BOTTLENOSE DOLPHIN

SEA OTTERS

SEA OTTER

Many sea otters spend their whole lives in the water. Their fur is water-repellent. This helps stop them from getting cold and wet while they swim around and float in the sea.

Sea otters often live in kelp forests near the coast. They sometimes tangle themselves up in kelp so that they do not get pushed around by the waves while they sleep.

CREATURES OF THE COAST

The coasts are home to many amazing animals. These creatures are all different and need different things. Coasts give these animals plenty of places to find food, stay safe, and look after their young.

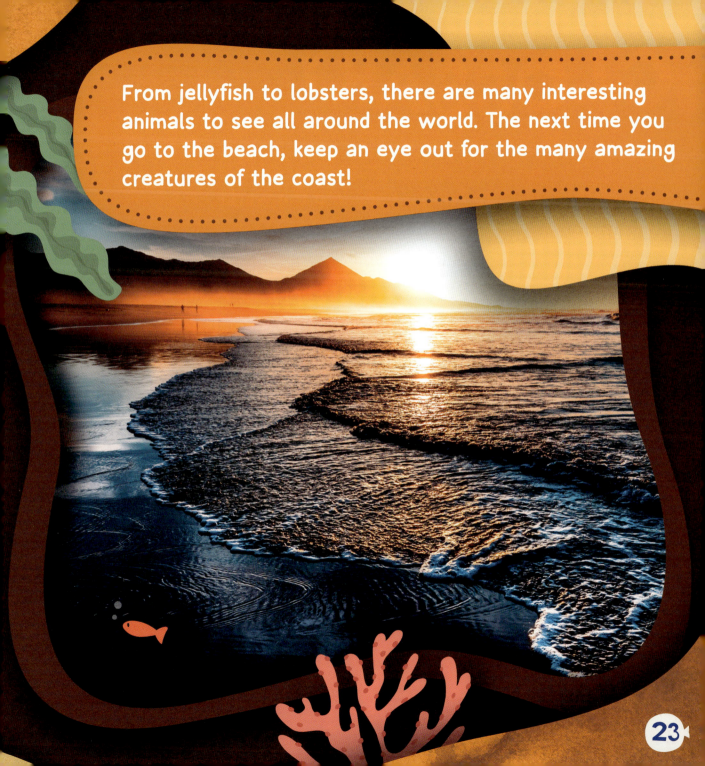

From jellyfish to lobsters, there are many interesting animals to see all around the world. The next time you go to the beach, keep an eye out for the many amazing creatures of the coast!

GLOSSARY

give birth — to bring a baby into the world

mammals — animals that are warm-blooded, have backbones, and produce milk

nurseries — safe places used to bring up young

predators — animals that hunt other animals for food

prey — animals that are eaten by other animals

shallow — not deep

shore — the land by the coast

skeletons — the framework of bones supporting the body

social — often found interacting with others in a group

water-repellent — able to stop water from making something too wet

INDEX

claws 14
fins 10, 16
food 5, 12, 14, 22
kelp 5, 21
seagrass 5, 11

sharks 13
shells 14–15
skeletons 6
water 4–5, 8, 12–13, 16, 18, 2
waves 9, 21